Shipping Container Homes:

30 Hacks For Beginners On Building Shipping Container Home

Table of content

Introduction

Some people might call it upcycling, and others would call it value-cycling. However you want to look at it, utilizing unused storage containers, to build a home, just makes good sense. It is actually better for the planet, less costly and easier to re-use the millions of unused containers taking up space across the world, than it is to completely recycle them.

Speaking of cost, you can purchase a single shipping container for around $2,000, depending on the type and size you choose, and if you purchase more than one. For instance, if you were to purchase more than one shipping container, you may be able to get a quantity discount.

Imagine; taking a huge metal shipping container, turning it into a comfortable and gorgeous home, and saving money while doing it!

Now you can unleash that imagination, because the "DIY Project: Shipping Container Homes: 30 Secret Tips How to Build Your Own Shipping Container Home!" guide is going to teach you everything you need to know.

Whether you are interested in creating a small living space out of one 8 feet wide, 40 feet long and 9 feet tall hunk of sturdy metal, or want to build a larger home by adding multiple metal boxes together, you are going to be thrilled when you hear how simple it is to do!

How simple, you may be wondering? Well, you can easily find the perfect shipping containers for your needs. For instance, you can even purchase them on eBay! They are currently available to "Buy Now" starting at $1,650. There are also mini containers included in design kits that you can purchase to help lay out your building plans.

There is really no limit to what you choose to include in your shipping container home. You may choose to install doors and windows, paneling or drywall and any type of flooring. And, of course you will want electric, plumbing, and a heating and cooling system. Ultimately, how much design and effort you put into your shipping container home is up to you.

What you need to get started is:

- The knowledge

- A plot of land

- Building permits per your city ordinance

- Tools, whether borrowed, rented or owned

- A plan

- Whatever materials you need to complete your plan

This guide will provide you with the knowledge and you can work on gathering everything else you as you complete the following chapters. To further help you complete a successful plan for your shipping container home, there are 30 secret tips from people who have already built homes.

Let's get started…

Chapter 1 – The Benefits of Using Shipping Containers

There are a number of personal and not so personal benefits for choosing to build your home using shipping containers. You may be a bit curious about why they are not being more widely used, or why they are suddenly becoming such a hot trend in architectural circles.

Shipping containers didn't come into existence until the 1960s. At that time, they were strictly for the use of making worldwide shipments between railroad, ships and tractor-trailers more efficient. The containers made it possible to quickly load and unload the containers from one mode of transportation to the next, without having to load and unload the contents they contained.

Over the next thirty years, these innovative shipping containers would gain heavier use as trade globalization increased significantly. These containers were built to withstand the brutal salty ocean climate while safely transporting up to 20 tons of products, from China to America and everywhere in between.

The structure of these containers has to withstand being lifted into a ship, off of a ship, onto and off of a rail car, and onto and off of a tractor-trailer, while they are filled to capacity. At the same time, the containers need to protect the contents from any type of damage. Because of this type of heavy use and requirements, they are some of the strongest structures built.

By 1999 there were more than 200 million shipping containers traveling to various locations. The average lifespan for use of these containers for shipping purposes is up to 8 years, with most of them being retired after two to three years. What this means today is that that millions of shipping containers are filling up stockyards all over the world.

Of course shipping containers can be recycled, but the energy needed for this is immense. Instead, if they can be upcycled, or value-cycled into providing housing, offices, and other types of buildings, then energy is saved and the ideal structure becomes available for even the most treacherous climates.

No other structure is known to withstand hurricanes, tornadoes and other dangerous weather conditions the same way that shipping containers are able to. They are also waterproof and unsusceptible to pests such as termites. They also won't break down as easily as brick and mortar buildings do after many years of being exposed to the elements.

Because there are so many millions of empty shipping containers overflowing stockyards and seaports, they are readily available for use. And, because of the supply and demand equation, they are very affordable for anyone who wishes to purchase them.

These containers are built with the toughest of corrugated steel, with tubular steel frames. They come equipped with marine grade flooring and locking steel doors that are vandal proof. The welded seams on these containers are water resistant and they are built to stack easily one upon the other. In fact, when they are stacked together, they offer even more strength and durability.

Along with strength, availability, affordability, and the opportunity to recreate these shipping containers into a home that will withstand extreme weather and the test of time, they make it easy to quickly build any type of home you want to live in. Nothing else on earth offers this many benefits for someone who dreams of building their own home.

Chapter 2 – Types of Shipping Containers

You might be surprised to learn that there are over fifty different styles of shipping containers available. Not all of these styles are suitable for use in building your home with though. For instance, open top containers which have an open top and opening sides do not have the type of strong structural foundation you need.

Another type of container that you will not want as part of your home is a tank container. These are the large cylinder shaped containers that are used for shipping liquids, including the most hazardous variety. For obvious reasons, unless you want to live in a round home, it would not make sense to invest in this type of shipping container.

Insulated containers, sometimes referred to as thermal containers have insulation, although this is not the type you want for your home. These generally have temporary types of insulation, such as gels. Refrigeration containers, also called reefers have a unit installed to keep items frozen or cooled and these are not the type you want to use for your home either.

Then there are the intermodal container collections of shipping containers. These are the type that are used for building homes. These are also called dry freight containers, cube containers, insulated containers, and ocean containers. If this type of container has a taller ceiling, it is called a high cube container.

The intermodal containers are one structures that opens from the front only, which give them the structural strength that's perfect for building a sturdy home.

If they are dry freight containers, they will not have insulation and are used for shipping dry goods and other types of products which do not need temperature considerations.

You may also hear of these types of containers being called:

- ISO Container, (International Standards Organization)
- Cargo container
- Conex box
- GreenCube
- ISBU, (Intermodal Steel Building Unit)
- ISBU module
- Ocean container
- Sea container
- Shipping container
- Storage container

The size of the intermodal containers vary in lengths from 20 to 53 feet in length and then 8 feet wide and 8.6 feet high, unless it is a high cube which will be about a foot taller. Remember, the high cube style will have about one foot added to the height, which is typically coveted for having the additional ceiling space.

Shipping Container Dimensions:

- 20 foot: up to 1,165 cubic square feet, which equals about 133 square feet interior space.
- 40 foot: up to 2,350 cubic feet with about 273 square feet of interior space.
- 45 foot: up to 3,043 cubic feet with about 308 square feet of interior space.
- 48 foot: up to 3,454 cubic feet with about 376 square feet of interior space.
- 53 foot: up to 3,857 cubic feet with about 416 square feet of interior space.

Knowing the type and size of container is best for building your house will become very important as you start to shop for them, especially if you are shopping through resources such as eBay. Remember, you can buy more than one in order to have the amount of interior square feet that you want for your home.

Chapter 3 – Shipping Container Home Plans

Now that you know what type of shipping containers and the sizes that are available, you can begin to consider plans for how to use them to create your new home. There is no limit to the amount of configurations you can come up with in order to create the type of home you have always dreamed of, whether you use one container or more.

If you are interested in tiny home living, then one container will suit you beautifully. This will give you enough space to create either a studio style or one bedroom home. You can then add a bathroom and kitchenette and decorate in your favorite colors and textures. As you have probably guessed, one container homes are the quickest and easiest to build.

For a studio style or one bedroom home, you can use a 20 foot, up to 53 foot container and determine where you want a wall, or walls for the bathroom. You can also choose if you want to keep a wide open living space, or create an additional wall or walls to block off a bedroom. Once you have made those choices, you will be able to know where to cut for windows, if you want them.

Along with having your layout in advance so you can choose where to cut for windows, you will also want to know how and where to run electrical wires and plumbing. Some homes also use gas for heating and if you will be using this utility, then you will want to plan for it accordingly as well.

You may want a larger home and how you use multiple shipping containers to build it is only limited by your imagination, your budget and the amount of land you have. For example, you may put two trailers side by side flush against each other, or build three containers into a U-Shape and build your home that way.

Containers can be stacked if you want multiple floors or very high ceilings. You can stack them flush, or set one trailer to face north to south and stack one on top like a crisscross, facing east to west.

The most important thing to remember is to plan to build a strong foundation to set your home on. A concrete slab is the most durable, but you can also use concrete posts or create a crawl space or even a basement. In this guide, we will talk about using a concrete slab.

As mentioned in a previous chapter, there are kits you can buy that will help you create your own home plans. These kits come with miniature containers, grid paper and suggestions so you can build a tiny model of the home before you begin to build it.

You can also download shipping container home design software such as ContainerHome3D. This software allows you to create a three dimensional image of your plans. It has everything you need, including foundation, roof, materials, windows, doors and more.

If you do not feel creative, you can just purchase ready-made plans that will tell you exactly what you need to build any style and size home you like. Some of these plans come along with pre-cut shipping containers and other types of materials you need to get the job done.

Before finalizing your building plans, make sure to check with your local building codes for rules and regulations. Some neighborhoods have strict requirements on square footage and other details that could affect your overall plans.

Chapter 4 – How to Purchase Shipping Containers

When you have finalized your building plans and made sure that you will be able to get the correct building permits, then you can start to shop for all the materials you will need. While it is easy to find most of these materials at your local hardware stores, you cannot buy shipping containers there.

Fortunately, finding the perfect shipping container for your needs is simple. You already know that you can find them on eBay, and if you shop there, please make sure that you research the seller. This is important because not everyone selling items on eBay have your best interest in mind.

You can buy prefabricated containers that are already cut and prepared for whatever plan you have in mind. Or, you can go straight to the manufacturer. Globalspec.com has ISO qualified manufacturer listings.

Many shipping container manufacturers will sell both used and new containers. Another directory to find container manufacturers is the National Portable Container Association. This association can also help you find shipping methods and custom fittings if you need them to complete your plan.

Shopping Considerations:

- If you want new or nearly new containers, look for those labeled "one trip". These shipping containers have only been used for one shipment and will be as close to new as possible.

- If you live near the ocean, you will want containers that are made out of corten steel. This is the best type of steel to stand up to the salty climate in regard to avoiding rust.

- If you do not intend to insulate or cover the exterior of your containers, then you will want to look for "no shipping label" containers. They will be painted, but will not have any type of labels or brand logos on them.

- Speaking of paint, if you want a freshly painted container that hasn't been refurbished, look for "factory paint" containers. This will help you avoid problems from paint peeling.

- You will hear the term "wind-water-tight" which means that the container is considered waterproof and wind resistant. While these are desirable features for your container, it is better to look for "cargo worthy" containers as they have been inspected and approved, where not all "wind-water-tight" containers have that distinction.

- Beware of shipping containers for sale that are labeled "as-is". While you may get a great price on these type of used containers, they will often have dents, leaks or other undesirable features.

When you find the container, or containers, that have all the features you want, make sure there are no dents, rust spots and that the doors open and close properly. Also, be aware of odors as even in metal containers, those can be next to impossible to remove.

Chapter 5 – How to Build Your Shipping Container Home

When you have your plan, land, permits, and materials, you are ready to start building! Simply follow these 12 steps and you will be ready to move in and relax in the comfort of your new home before you know it!

1. The first thing to do is make sure that you have the land raised, flattened or otherwise ready to place a foundation upon. This may require bringing in fill dirt, or removing extra dirt and otherwise leveling the land.

2. When the land is ready, you can build a foundation and the best one is a concrete slab. That requires laying a frame to pour the concrete in. It is also helpful if you embed steel plates where the corner of the container blocks will be rested. This will create the firmest foundation for your home.

3. If you have never poured concrete, you will want to study this as there are important things to keep in mind, such as what type of weather to pour the concrete in and how to spread it properly.

4. When the foundation is complete, you can add the container, or containers. A crane is the best tool to use for positioning the containers on the foundation, but you can use swing-thru trucks or even a rough terrain forklift. Surprisingly, you can easily make any last minute adjustments to how your containers are resting on the foundation with a crowbar.

5. If you are using multiple containers, you will want to connect them together to keep the strongest possible structure for your home. You can use specialized clamps, bolts or weld the containers together. If you think you might take the

home apart someday to move it, then choose bolts instead of welding. Otherwise, welding will help you create a permanent structure.

6. After the containers are connected, you can add the reinforcements. While some reinforcements will have to wait until after you cut out the sides or windows, setting as many of the reinforcements ahead of time will preserve the structure while you make changes. For example, placing steel beams to strengthen the roof if you are cutting out entire walls from the container.

7. Before cutting windows, doors or walls out of the shipping containers, add the roof. If you are using the container roof, then you can skip this step. However, if you are cutting off the roof and building a new one, it is going to work out the best if you do this step after setting the reinforcements.

8. When the roof is in place, it is time to cut out the walls, windows and doors. Make sure that you have enough reinforcements in place as cutting into the walls of the structure will weaken it. If you have any doubts, consult with an engineer before completing this step.

9. After you have made the necessary cuts, you can either remove the flooring, or encapsulate it. Many shipping container home builders will have a professional do this part of the building process due to how the flooring has been treated with pesticides or other toxins. To use it as a sub-flooring, you can encapsulate it in epoxy. Otherwise, just remove it and add a new sub-flooring.

10. With the floor in place, seal any cracks around the windows, doors, and any other part of the container that you had cut into before enclosing the openings and putting in whatever walls are part of your plan. You are then ready to insulate the outside and add siding if that is part of your plan.

11. With the exterior completed, you can start to build the walls of the interior. Remember to consider the electrical, plumbing and heating lines that you will be running. Some people will add these lines before adding walls. Depending on your plan, you may want to add the utilities before you add walls, but that is up to you.

12. By the time you have added electric, plumbing and heating and walls, you are ready to add the final touches. From this point you can build in your kitchen and bathroom cabinets, and other furnishings. You can tile, carpet, paint or do any other final touches.

You may want to take before and after pictures of every step you take. You can use these if you run into any challenges. There are shipping containing builders or even general contractors who would be happy to help answer any questions you have.

Whether you build this home all by yourself or hire others for specific parts of the building process, such as the plumbing or heating, you should find that building with shipping containers is the quickest and easiest way to build your own home.

The next two chapters have some valuable information that you will want to make sure to review before you start the process of building your shipping container home.

Chapter 6 – Secret Tips 1 through 15

As promised, the next two chapters include 30 secrets to how to build your own shipping container home. They come from other people who have built homes by themselves and professionals in the field of architecture and construction.

These 15 secrets are best to keep in mind before purchasing shipping container home plans:

1. Consider taking adult classes on welding, plumbing or electric wiring instead of hiring professionals. Not only will you enjoy learning new skills, you will eventually save money on repairs, replacements and updates. Many community colleges offer classes that teach skills in a semester without having to go through an entire certification program.

2. Get your plans together for what type of home you want to build before you buy your land. This way you can discuss what the best piece of land will be with your real estate agent. Or, if you already own land, double check to see which plans you will be able to get permits for before investing too much money.

3. Never buy a container "sight un-seen". You may not like what you end up and it can be worth it to pay travel expenses if you have to in order to make sure the container you are purchasing is up to your expectations. Also, make sure you are buying from a reputable dealer.

4. Always negotiate for a reduced price. While between $1,600 and $2,000 is the typical going rate for standard shipping containers, you can oftentimes

get a reduced price if you are buying more than one. Or, you can negotiate for reduced moving rates to place the containers on your property.

5. Even if you have the plan you want to use for building your home, check it against the layout of the property and make sure each room is placed in the house in the best way possible. For instance, bedrooms should be as far away from the street as possible in order to cut down on noise.

6. Make any other adjustments to your home plans before you even lay the foundation. For instance, if you want rooms with southern exposure, then you will want to make sure to place the largest windows on the south side of your home.

7. Instead of paying expensive rental fees for equipment such as welding or other construction equipment, check with your local community development agency to see if they have reduced rate rentals or even "for free" lending programs for local residents.

8. Buy remnants whenever possible and stay in contact with your local contractors associations to learn about the best deals on materials. You can also place an ad in your local newspaper or Craigslist for the materials you are looking for. Someone who has too much may see the ad and sell to you at reduced costs.

9. When laying the foundation, build out a generous trench and fill it with gravel to make sure you have adequate drainage. For the best results,

create a six inch wide by 18 to 24 inch deep trench, line it, and fill it with the largest fill gravel possible.

10. Leave the container doors on. You can fit sliding glass doors in and still leave the container doors on in order to close for additional security or to protect from heavy storms and hurricanes.

11. Use double paned glass to help keep heat in or out, out of your container home. Also, caulk all the windows with waterproof caulk to get rid of any drafts.

12. Use white shades and heavy curtains to help keep container cooler in the summer. Planting trees for shade and opening windows at night and closing them before 8:00 am will help keep your home cooler without having to run an air conditioner.

13. For cold weather climates, use two or more layers of rigid insulation and then use offset joints and a fiber cement protection board to keep the trailer cozy.

14. Consider using radiant heating in your floor boards. Because heat rises, the warm floors will help keep the entire area warmer and keep other heating costs lower.

15. Consider insulating on the outside instead of on the inside to keep as much interior space as possible. Also, insulate all electrical outlets and anything else that you build into the walls.

Chapter 7 – Secret Tips 16 through 30

The following secrets will come in handy if you are aware of them before you start constructing your steel container home. This way you can build them into your planning:

16. Before doing any construction, have the containers professionally cleaned. If they had been treated with poisons to keep pests away, or hauled dangerous materials such as asbestos, it is best to count on professionals to remove every last trace of residue.

17. When cutting out the long sides of the container, make sure you add supporting elements such as beams to keep the structure strong.

18. Keep the metal from the parts of the container that you cut out. You can use them later in a variety of ways, such as framing them in wood and using them for a deck or patio wall. You can also use them inside to create shelving or outside to create an awning or gardening containers.

19. Create shelves underneath each step of a staircase and underneath the staircase to maximize the use of space when building a two story container home.

20. Use PEX instead of rigid plumbing PVC for plumbing. It holds up better and can easily be bent by heating it up.

21. For an ultra-modern look, sandblast the paint from the inside of the container and allow the bare steel to develop a patina. This should be done

before you do anything else because it will be much easier to clean the mess up.

22. Using old barn wood can help soften the hardness of stainless steel in the bathroom if you prefer more traditional styles.

23. Consider adding solar panels as an alternative energy source.

24. Choose an energy efficient toilet and other plumbing accessories to help save water.

25. Bamboo plywood is sustainable and can be used for flooring and for paneling if you do not want container exposed interior walls.

26. Use a plasma cutter to cut out the windows and door frames. It melts the metal along with cutting and you don't have to replace the parts as often as you do with other types of cutting tools.

27. Really consider the plan you choose and do not be afraid to change it around to better fit your lifestyle. For instance, if the kitchen layout is not to your liking, it is easier to change before you run the plumbing and electrical lines than trying to change it after the fact.

28. If you get stuck doing it yourself, see if you can barter services with someone else in your area who is building a storage container home.

29. If you cut off the top of the storage container to add a different type of roof, make sure you have framing for ample support for the additional weight of whatever type of roof you add.

30. Memorize all the measurements from zero to one inch, down 1/16 because everything you will be cutting will have to be extremely accurate. This will save a great deal of time and frustration from having to stop and count or convey to your building partner if you have one.

Conclusion

Even if you had never heard of using shipping containers to build homes before reading the DIY Project: Shipping Container Homes: 30 Secret Tips How to Build Your Own Shipping Container Home!" guide, you now have all the knowledge you need to get started building a home of your own that you will enjoy for years to come.

Just think, not only can you do something healthy for the planet to upcycle, or value cycle what is otherwise creating a problem, but you can affordably, quickly and easily build any type of home you want!

Here is a quick list of what you learned for easy reference as you begin to make up the dreams for your new home:

- What types of shipping containers are available and which ones are the best to purchase for building a home.
- Where to purchase shipping containers and specific considerations to help you choose the best one.
- What types of designs you can make to use in building your home, and where to find the tools that will help you create your plan.
- 12 steps to building your shipping container home.
- 30 secret tips to help you build the home of your dreams.

Soon you will be able to find out for yourself how quickly, easily and affordably you can build any size shipping container home you like.

Best wishes as you create a home that you and your family will love for years to come!

Made in United States
Troutdale, OR
09/06/2023

12665691R00015